Public
Figures

Wesleyan Poetry

Public Figures

Jena Osman

WESLEYAN UNIVERSITY PRESS

MIDDLETOWN, CONNECTICUT

Wesleyan University Press
Middletown CT 06459
www.wesleyan.edu/wespress
© 2012 Jena Osman
All rights reserved
Manufactured in the
United States of America
Designed & typeset by
Sara Rutan in Warnock Pro

Wesleyan University Press
is a member of the Green Press Initiative.
The paper used in this book meets their
minimum requirement for
recycled paper.

Library of Congress
Cataloging-in-Publication Data
Osman, Jena
Public figures / by Jena Osman.
p. cm.—(Wesleyan poetry)
ISBN 978-0-8195-7311-7 (cloth: alk. paper)—
ISBN 978-0-8195-7312-4 (ebook)
I. Title.
PS3565.S6P83   2012
811.54—dc23
2012012530

5 4 3 2

Monuments today should do what we all
have to do, make more of an effort! Anybody
can stand quietly by the side of the road and
allow glances to be bestowed on him; these
days we can demand more of monuments.

—ROBERT MUSIL, "MONUMENTS"

There are things
We live among "and to see them
Is to know ourselves"

—GEORGE OPPEN, "OF BEING NUMEROUS"

Public
Figures

How did it occur?

Was it this:

> One day, quite some time ago, I happened on a photograph
> of Napoleon's youngest brother, Jerome, taken in 1852. And
> I realized then, with an amazement I have not been able
> to lessen since: "I am looking at eyes that looked at the
> Emperor."
> —ROLAND BARTHES, *CAMERA LUCIDA*

Or was it this:

> If you could see what I've seen with your eyes . . .
> —ROY BATTY, *BLADE RUNNER*

Or was it this:

> Pausing before an 18th-century church cemetery you look
> through the locked gate. There, on a small hill, is a life-sized
> statue of the Virgin Mary. Her gaze rests on an enormous
> red and white banner for an athletic club franchise across
> the street.

The idea occurred:

Photograph the figurative statues that populate your city. Then bring the camera to their eyes (find a way) and shoot their points of view. What does such a figure see?

To see the sigh of sighted stone you activate the idea.

You find a way, jerry-rig an apparatus made from a mop handle, a disposable camera with a timer, some velcro tape.

Out in the field, you observe and take notes. You set the timer and pull the pin.

Erected in 1884 and located on the north side of Philadelphia's City Hall, this statue of Major John Fulton Reynolds was the city's first equestrian statue and first public monument in honor of a Civil War soldier. Reynolds was from Lancaster, killed at Gettysburg, and his nickname was "Old Common Sense."

possible new target   approaching target one building
designate new target   target five   pilot copies   sensor

And here is what he's looking at:

Reynolds was very well respected, but his career had few suc-
cesses. For instance, once after two long days of battle, he fell
asleep under a tree and was taken prisoner for six weeks. Was
that tree like this tree? Is Reynolds being forced to look at an
emblem of what was perhaps his greatest embarrassment? You'd
like to get back in the air.

copies   white pickup arrived in front of target building
pilot copy   two passengers including target five have

Next to Reynolds is another Civil War soldier, General George McClellan. McClellan was considered a good organizer, but not a particularly good general. He had a variety of nicknames, such as "The Young Napoleon," "Mac the Unready," and—because of his reluctance to attack—"The Little Corporal of Unsought Fields."

entered the building from the white pickup   confirmed
target in building   copy   sensor confirms   if possible

He looks out and sees:

You yourself are a patch-wearer; you are committed to your job.

keep eyes on building and pickup   building has the
priority   pilot mc, in order to do that I need tail 107 to

Most figurative sculptures are clustered along the river drive that is part of Frederick Law Olmsted's Fairmount Park. From their pedestals they have lovely static views of the river and trees.

They loom above you. You map out a rescue plan.

come off its current target   get permission for 107 to
come south   copy and censor   leave the bridge locked

When you are out there with the camera apparatus, it takes passersby a minute to understand what you are doing. But when they do—the moment when they realize that these figures indeed have a gaze projected outward—they gasp and laugh. Immobile, you watch it all the way to impact.

locked up until we get permission to come off that target
roger wilco   pilot mc cleared off target censor   you can

For the most part, the sculptures seem to be looking at nothing in particular; they have a gaze, but they don't have a need for it. You wonder about your experiment, whether it has any value at all. You wind up and throw it in the air.

break lock on the bridge and lock up the target five with
tail 107   roger   we've got 60 degrees more of hitting

While proceeding, you become aware of your *not* noticing. You walk around these figures as if they are buildings or large pieces of furniture. You navigate their boundaries without a momentary meditation on who they are or why they're there. With that public invisibility in mind, you become aware that a fair number of these statues populating your city are armed.

copy pilot   I've got eight missiles and two bombs on two predators in the target vicinity   target five leaving

Story: Instructions come in a blue envelope carefully sealed and stamped with the word "government." Use a letter opener and slide it inside the fold, cutting cleanly across as you've been taught to do. Your gloves leave no prints.

Image:
You kneel with knees in the mud.
As if a cloud were just a set of lines, manmade and fierce.
A thing, eyes to the sky and hands outstretched.
You see yourself as a cliché, just a body beneath the stars and
    open to the elements.

Caption: A couple arm in arm. Three pass. Two pass. Now three now one. Man in shirt sleeves. Man with bag slung over shoulder. Sad presentiments of what must come to pass.

Story: The mission is already dead in the water. If it hadn't been for a lucky break (which you failed to mention in your report) you might not be where you are today. The mission part is difficult. It requires a certain language, the language of dispersal and direction. It requires following orders without really understanding ultimate goals. It requires endurance and a cheery heart.

Image:
Bayonets and daggers.
The men in uniform with their flat hats and scabbards, their
    knapsacks and greatcoats.
The men without hats in their street clothes and high socks,
    drooling blood.
The woman behind the knee, the child below the knee, the man
    who sets the knife to the child.
Can one sharpened pole win against manufactured arms?
A people and their poles, with or without reason.

Caption: Woman hunched over in red sweater getting into white suv with younger, taller woman. Man with pin-striped pants. With or without reason.

Story: It has dawned on you that although you're intimately familiar with every crease in the map, you're not entirely sure of where you're going. You look for clues as to what you may be looking for. You set in motion some investigations, a thing among things. At the moment, the results are not particularly interesting—not nearly as interesting as the idea itself. But maybe there's something you're not seeing . . . You tear up the floorboards. You hide the telephone in a drawer. You carry the evidence in a blue plastic envelope and clutch it to your chest.

Image:
The long rope taut over the shoulder.
The knots around the ankles of the other.
The man as sheepskin on the back of the long rope, deserving.
The weight of the body as it's dragged.
A man raises his baton.
A shadow behind the sheepskin points the unsheathed sword.

Caption: Two women pulling rolling luggage. Two men running. Woman on phone. Man on bike. He deserved it.

This statue depicts the Nordic explorer Thorfinn Karlsefni. He landed in North America in 1010 or maybe it was 1004, following hot on Leif Ericson's discovery of the magical land of Vinland, or Wineland, or was it Grassland? He landed although nobody really knows where . . . it was somewhere between Newfoundland and Virginia. He created a settlement that for a variety of reasons, including internal dissension, desertion, and native attacks, lasted a mere three years. Over nine centuries later, at the beginning of World War I, the sculptor Einar Jónsson was brought from Iceland to Philadelphia to make this sculpture. There are no actual images of Karlsefni, so this work is an imaginary rendition based on a bleary set of facts, a commissioned animation in a time of war. Your streaming data needs to be nimble.

building entering pickup   pickup now has priority

pilot copies   censor copies   pilot signal restriction

You stand quietly by the side of the road.

Perhaps the greatest work by the Scottish poet and sculptor Ian Hamilton Finlay is his garden, Little Sparta. This pastoral space is filled with words captioning walls, gates, trees, sundials, buildings, and bridges: "wave" "little fields long" "there is happiness" "azure & son / islands LTD / oceans inc." "nuclear sail."

In an essay on Little Sparta, Susan Stewart writes that in this garden "all space has been made semantic space."

cleared hot on white pickup   pilot spinup a weapon on
tail 107   copy   prelaunch checklist   prf code entered

In contrast, if your city and its sculptures are a kind of garden (can it be called a war garden?), it is a garden that has lost its semantic drive. These carefully designed emblems of wars past—symbols of values and virtues defended by spears and sabers—register only with the occasional tourist. The figures wait for your demands. Screens sweep you into their petrified world.

AEA power on   AEA bit in progress   passed weapon
power on   weapon bit passed code   weapons coded

You wonder how a weapon, and the body that carries it, can become so neutralized—to the point where you no longer take it in.

In the Arcades Project, Walter Benjamin wrote "The new, dialectical method of doing history presents itself as the art of experiencing the present as waking world." At this point it's an old idea that you can understand the past only from the standpoint of the present. You understand a place, a person, an action, not from what has been recorded, but from what has fallen out of the picture, forgotten. The historical fact is a double vision: tumbling into the present, it picks itself up and walks quickly away—at first flashing, clashing, then disappearing into the crowd. You take a sample, test the residue. You are the sensor.

weapons status   weapons ready   prelaunch checklist
complete   pilot signal   you are cleared to engage

The base for the Washington Grays monument was begun in 1872; the bronze figure was added in 1908. After four moves, the statue now stands in front of the Union League on Broad Street. The inscription reads "To Our Fallen Comrades 1861–1866."

As part of the Pennsylvania volunteer regiment during the Civil War, the Washington Grays Artillery Corp was one of the first groups to arrive in Washington at Lincoln's call, fully armed and ready for action. Most of the men were members of Philadelphia's elite class, then to be recast in stone. You stay with the program.

white pickup truck at your discretion   pilot cleared to engage white pickup truck   it looks like it's on the move

The Smithsonian Inventory of American Sculpture states that the Washington Grays monument was the brainchild of Edwin North Benson, a former member of the Gray Reserves, who donated $2,000 in 1871 toward its creation. As a wealthy and prominent member of postwar Philadelphia society (he was a banker before the war and an insurance magnate afterwards), he had the money to fund such memorials.

Benson was also a veteran of the Collis Zouaves d'Afrique, 114th Pennsylvania Volunteers. The Civil War Zouave soldiers were modeled after the French Zouaves, who themselves were modeled after Berbers in northern Algeria from the Zouaoua tribe. In the 1830s, the Berbers had been hired by the French to help them colonize North Africa. They became part of the occupying forces in Algeria and were known for their particularly aggressive fighting style.

Eventually the French replaced all of the Berber soldiers-for-hire with Frenchmen who called themselves the Zouaves. They adopted the Zouaoua style of dress, which included baggy pants, a sash, a short embroidered jacket and a tasseled red fez. You are suited up.

launch checklist   mts autotrack   established laser
laser selected   go ahead and arm your laser   laser's

During the Crimean War, Captain McClellan (later to be General McClellan of the Civil War or "the Little Corporal of Unsought Fields"), saw the French Zouaves in action. He considered the Zouaves to be ideal soldiers and brought their method and fashion back to the United States. Thus, the Civil War Union soldiers, while purportedly fighting against slavery, adopted the outfits of the French colonizers of North Africa. You are half-way around the world in a trailer.

armed   master arm is hot   go ahead and fly the laser
lasing within range   3 2 1 rifle   3 2 1 impact

Zouave uniforms were used to reward Union army regiments for exceptional battlefield performance. While Zouave units proliferated, the Zouave style started a fashion craze, influencing women and children's clothing.

On the field, the Civil War Zouave uniforms quickly wore out and the U.S. government refused to replace them due to the expense. Your outer skin, your inner skin, is metal.

go out into the field   set the lens   observe and take notes   report your findings   3 2 1 rifle   3 2 1

However, the style lives on thanks to groups such as the Collis Zouave reenactors at Gettysburg. Their website asks:

> Do you want to be authentic, but also portray a zouave? Are you tired of "progressive" and "campaigner" meaning you can only wear blue? If so, you have come to the right place. We want to show the reenacting community that you CAN be a zouave and still have the highest authenticity standards!
>
> It would be our hope that you or someone you know would like to join our living monument to the original 114th . . .

You are a rotating sphere of optics.

impact   possible new target   was that tree like this tree
confirmed   sensor confirms   3 2 1 rifle   3 2 1 impact

A year or so before Edwin Benson joined the Gray Reserves, Baudelaire wrote "The Painter of Modern Life." The "Military Man" section of the essay catalogs the variety of military uniforms in such detail that war reads as a kind of fashion show.

No matter the costume, Baudelaire notes the common element shared by all of the soldiers (including the Zouaves):

> Here we can see that uniformity of expression which is created by suffering and obedience endured in common, that resigned air of courage which has been put to the test by long, wearisome fatigues.

You get spun and then called back.

excellent job   two individuals and they're digging
around in the ground   looks like it   appears he's

This photo, by Max Becherer, appeared in the *New York Times* on February 5, 2006. The accompanying article by Dexter Filkins states:

> A group of about 20 uniformed Iraqi men, with a prisoner in its possession, was halted at a checkpoint. The men were wearing the telltale camouflage outfits of the police commandos . . . They seemed legitimate.
>
> But, after some checking, the Iraqis manning the checkpoint discovered that the men were not commandos after all. They were taking their prisoner to be shot.

covering something up   he's on the east side of the road
roger   there's a child just outside of that tent   the

The caption beneath the photo says "CAMOUFLAGE It's hard, in Iraq, to tell an enemy from an enemy's enemy. A villager can be an insurgent; a uniform can hide loyalty to a militia; a terrorist group can change its name."

There is something you're not seeing and you can sense it buzzing in the atmosphere as you stand quietly by the side of the road. Are you making progress? What do you shoot, save, rescue, aid, or err in this process?

individual wearing white is underneath that cover
we've identified a motorcycle with a barrel on it

Story: Is there a way to wake up? Light reaches in before you're ready and the envelope already awaits. You hold it in your hand and for a moment imagine not opening it, just walking away: a true improvisatory device. But the thought of breaking the routine that has held your life together for the past few years is more than you can bear.

Image:
The closed fist, the open hand.
The butcher wields his axe with skulls in his sleeves.
The flat hats are dying, the daggers win against the scabbards and swords.
The boots, the short pants unbuttoned at the calf.
The high-waisted belted support, a certain attire that speaks, arms above the head.
Everything the same to the upper right: the arm that holds the dagger, the hand that tries to stop the blow, the axe above the head before it crashes down.

Caption: Woman on phone. Two women walking and talking. Man with books and brown paper bag opening black car door looking at parking meter. The same.

Story: You begin the day with a brisk step and sense of purpose. But as soon as you meet the first stopping point in your delivered set of coordinates, you find yourself pausing too long. Long enough to give away the farm. So you push yourself along before your task is done, so as not to give yourself away.

Image:
Thinly masked critiques at the end of the disasters.
The leader as bishop is a hawk with heads sutured at the ends
     of each wing.
With knees in the mud.
The parrot, the ass, the dog, the monkey, the wolf.
Infantalized humanoids, all cower in their bestial cover behind
     the leader like a cloud, his wings holding back their perfidy
     of which he is a part.
You are the shadow at the back, looming like a trace of escape.

Caption: Man with safety orange sweater looking in backpack, then putting it on back. Man running while on cell phone. Family of three. Troupe of charlatans.

Story: The mission is like a caption that underlines all things. There are no trips to the grocery store without you thinking "I'm *performing* the act of shopping at the grocery store while in fact I'm fulfilling the terms of my contract." Sometimes you imagine yourself the hero so the more mundane aspects of your job seem filled with possibility.

Image:
In the foreground four dead men.
Three are naked, their clothes being ripped from them by the
    ones in sashes.
One man's head barely has features like a cartoon; another man
    dead with sideburns and a muscular chest.
Bodies collect around a tree, clumped by the roots.
The moustaches of the ones with sashes, the hilts of their
    swords.
Garments pulled over the head, pulled down to the ankles.
The broken tree limbs, the vague mountain.

Caption: Young woman in beach hat and thigh-high boots. Woman running with headphones. A couple holding hands. They avail themselves.

You look out and see:

Holding a golden sword and an enormous Bible, Johnnie Ring stands on a high pedestal behind the faculty club at Temple University in North Philadelphia. On one side of the pedestal is a long inscription:

> Johnnie Ring was the youth whose example in life and heroism in death provided inspiration that led to the founding of Temple University. In the war between the states, he was personal orderly to captain Russell H. Conwell of the 46th Massachusetts infantry. The moving forces of his life at that time were his religious faith and his devotion to Captain Conwell. When a surprise attack routed Union troops . . .

whatever he's covering in there   my only concern is
that child right now   once he gets away I'm good with it

. . . it was Johnnie Ring who raged across a flaming bridge and through enemy gunfire to retrieve from his commander's tent the ceremonial sword presented to the captain by the city of Springfield. He brought back the sword, but he died that night of his burns as Conwell knelt by his cot in prayer. The incident turned Conwell to the ministry as a life work and later to the founding of Temple University. He vowed to live a life for Johnnie Ring as well as for himself . . . eight hours of work a day for Johnnie, eight hours of work for his own. Except for Johnnie Ring, Conwell would never have told America the story of the acres of diamonds, nor would he have built the University that enabled multitudes of young men and women to realize the promise of that story.

Like Coleridge's ancient mariner, Conwell told the story of Johnnie Ring compulsively. However, evidence shows that Ring actually died of tuberculosis six weeks after the attack in question. In addition, on the day of Johnnie's death, Conwell was under military arrest and in the middle of a court-martial for being completely absent during that attack. He was charged with "shamefully abandoning his command in the face of the enemy."

roger   the child will be a concern   I understand that
this entire group has been involved in diverting traffic

As clear as the hypocrisies of the story show themselves to be, you find yourself returning again and again to the inscripted contradiction before your eyes.

A gift made in 1964 (the year the Vietnam war escalated in earnest) by the Temple University class of 1958, the message is ambivalent, needs to have it both ways. You're not sure of your name anymore.

away from that site where we saw them covering up the
IED tracks   what we're really waiting on now is 429 and

Conwell was a master rhetorician. His speeches and sermons were so popular that tickets were necessary for admission. In his rambling lecture "Acres of Diamonds" (written in 1900 and delivered more than 6,000 times across the United States—you can find it on Temple's website), Conwell praised the goodness of the robber barons and questioned the legitimacy of organized labor. He urged his audiences

> to spend time getting rich. You and I know there are some things more valuable than money; of course, we do. . . . Nevertheless, the man of common sense also knows that there is not any one of those things that is not greatly enhanced by the use of money. Money is power.

And so, as the faculty of Temple University line up for the salad bar and lunch buffet in the Diamond Club, they can look out the window and see Johnnie (Johnny) Ring holding Conwell's ceremonial sword and perhaps meditate on what he represents. Are they like Johnnie Ring, loyal to the death to their captain Conwell? Or are they simply eating lunch?

for the child to move   all right   those individuals now
are where that IED is suspected   two individuals, one on the

---

And how many of them have looked at this sculpture close enough to notice how the middle finger of Johnnie Ring's hand is clearly a prosthetic, obscenely exaggerated in order to hold up the weight of what it carries.

In the belly, in the clouds, no fixed orbit. You fly a hexagon.

motorcycle one off the motorcycle where they're digging
it up   they're working on the road   they're digging

The only armed figurative monument to post–Civil War dead in Philadelphia is posted at 2nd and Spring Garden Streets.

According to the Smithsonian Inventory database, it is called "Spirit of the American Doughboy," created by Ernest Moore Viquesney. It is the most reproduced life-sized statue in the United States. One hundred and thirty-nine of them are known to exist (there are probably more), and they're scattered all over the country. As the Smithsonian inventory describes it, all of these sculptures have the same characteristics: an upwardly extended right arm with a grenade in the upraised hand, a left arm extended downward holding a bayoneted rifle pointed forward at about thigh height, a flat steel helmet, wrapped leggings below the knees, two tree stumps by the feet and the leading left leg is straight.

around that same area   they've positioned themselves on
the opposite side of that motorcycle   they're definitely

Two tree stumps by the feet and the leading left leg is straight. Your photographic evidence does not match up with the database, which sets off alarms.

In trying to get to the bottom of the discrepancy, you find yourself in the labyrinth of Earl Goldsmith's *Spirit of the American Doughboy* website looking for clues. Was the Philadelphia doughboy an anonymous knock-off? You send Mr. Goldsmith a query and within twenty-four hours receive a lengthy response.

digging in the road   is that a kid   dammit!   the kid
appears to be carrying something over to the vicinity

Apparently the Smithsonian database has it wrong; Philadelphia's sculpture is actually called "Over the Top" by John Paulding. According to Mr. Goldsmith, both Paulding and Viquesney registered similar designs for copyright in 1920, but Paulding did so about six months before Viquesney. In fact, in 1922, Viquesney was sued for copyright infringement by Paulding's foundry. But the suit must not have been successful, for Visquesney's sculptures continued to proliferate, and advertisements for Visquesny's version—clearly with Paulding's sculptures in mind—urged buyers to purchase the "authentic" doughboy, because there's "just one accurate authentic Doughboy Statue . . . Don't Be Fooled."

The authentic multiple. The sporadic identical. The auratic mechanical. Can you hide the sounds of your propellers?

digging up that road   we're at 2700   that individual's
moving with a wheelbarrow in the same area   looks like

Story: The cause keeps you going although if you're asked to explain it you claim you don't know what it is. You're only a foot soldier in a continuing drama, the limits of which are always kept slightly out of reach. You're not a runner. Your reputation is built on your willingness to bring a job to completion.

Image:
The characters are praying before the bayonets.
Rather the ends of the bayonets, the points appearing from
    out-of-frame as narrow sharks.
Hands clasped at chest, hands clasped before the kneeling
    body.
Hands clasping a robed figure.
Hands open to the sky in a faint.
Hands hiding the eyes.
Hands empty against the floorboards.

Caption: A man with two dogs on leashes. A woman with a small shopping bag. A group of individuals in a line. One cannot look at this.

Story: You've been evaluating your options. On the one hand, all has gone according to plan. On the other hand, you feel yourself losing your motivation, your focus. The data set is missing a crucial page, buried at the scene. Focus on what matters: Timing. Persistence. Clarity of purpose. The landscape is secondary.

Image:
At the fairground or a water wheel, reflection dipping with the
    sun.
The woman in white and the woman with a dagger.
The woman in white with her fingers as a claw, scratching
    against the face of another.
The woman with the knife ready to plunge into the other.
The other a face with a grin and moustache, a Cossack's hat
    and hilt at the knee.
Hiding her face behind her arm's interior.

Caption: Cement mixer. Chain link fence. Vinyl screen. Porta-Potties. Trucks, trailers, cranes & dumpsters. Tour buses. "Beautiful flowers." Bare trees. They do not want to.

Story: You ask yourself "am I making progress? what do I accomplish, save, rescue, aid or err in this process?" You wonder if you can possibly initiate a positive condition or if your job is really a part of the problem. Internal questioning is a constant set-up. You set the timer and pull the pin.

Image:
A man runs forward with a sack under his arm.
All other eyes look off to the right in fear.
A soldier points off to the right, his left hand tries to ward off
    the invisible.
A woman with a baby over her shoulder.
The woman lifts her child from the ground.
The woman leans forward, the soldier backward.
A crowd running over the hill.
Are they happy? Are they frightened? Are they friend or foe?

Caption: In a trailer just outside of Las Vegas. If you could see what I've seen. Around the corners and over hills. I saw it.

In her essay "Sculpture in the Expanded Field," Rosalind Kraus writes of monuments such as these (figurative, vertical, with prominent pedestals) as speaking "in a symbolical tongue about the meaning or use of a place," but that late in the 19th century, a kind of sitelessness or "loss of place" took over and the logic of the monument began to fade.

These men without a home, without a site to call their own. You enter coordinates and see airspace.

he went down to get water   he's continuing back to get
more water or something   the child brought something

---

without a site to call your own
to see the frame that blinds
to see the sigh in sighted stone
the stone to call the lime to blind

without a sight to call your own
to see the frame that blinds
to wander through the weary dead
to take a sword to neck and head

to the two individuals   at this point are you confident
that you have ID   roger   I believe that's a hostile act

The fact is these monuments moved around.

The Washington Grays sculpture started off at the intersection of Broad and Girard (1872). It was then moved to Washington Square (1898), subsequently transferred to Fairmount Park on Lemon Hill Drive (1954), and finally landed in front of the Union League (1991).

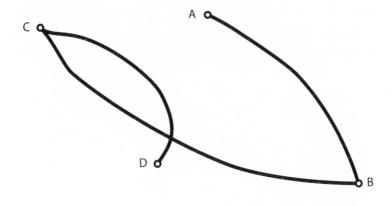

that's in the same area that we saw them cover   roger
copy   it just detonated by itself   they just blew

Finished in 1877, the sculpture "Stone Age in America" was shipped from France, to be shown at the American Art Association exhibition in New York City. When it arrived in Philadelphia, it was exhibited at the Haseltine and Company gallery, then stood temporarily outside the post office at Ninth and Chestnut until it was installed near Sweetbriar Mansion in West Fairmount Park in 1888. In 1893 it was sent to Chicago for the World's Columbian Exposition, after which it returned to the Sweetbriar Mansion area until 1985, when it was relocated to a grassy plot near Boathouse Row.

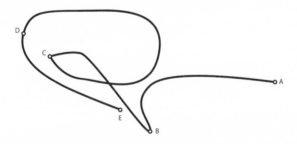

it just detonated by itself   they just blew themselves up
they apparently just blew themselves up

Are you losing your place?

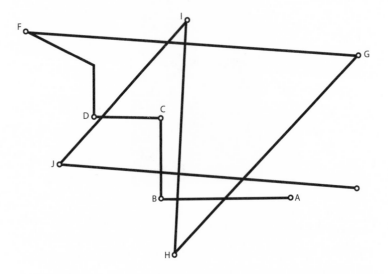

You track your own coordinates as you move from base to platform, the mobile plinth.

tracking   I got the square building and the rectangle
building   to the northwest   we have a square building

Ian Hamilton Finlay's "Man with Panzerschreck" modifies a copy of a classical statue (which made its way via replication from Greece to Rome to the British Museum to Little Sparta) so that the young athlete casually holds a German anti-tank rocket launcher from World War II. Finlay's garden also contains warships, grenades, panzer helmets, minesweepers. An Apollo with a machine gun in his hand instead of a lyre.

In an interview, Finlay said, "It is quite a natural process to use other times to understand your own time. It offers a kind of dramatic possibility or something like that. Of course our time does not try to understand itself at all, unfortunately . . ."

and a rectangle building to the northwest   now on the
big square building there's a square rectangular holding

Susan Stewart writes that

> Finlay's garden as a paradise of philosophy constantly
> reminds us of the agon between forms of thought, the sim-
> plemindedness of monumentality, and the fragile boundary
> between art and war. . . . The garden refuses to allow the
> viewer to identify naively with its individual themes and
> symbols; Finlay argues that when individuals pursue an un-
> thinking identification with power and sentimental ideals,
> terror and catastrophe ensue.

You become aware of your *not* noticing. You wind up and throw
it in the air. A raven. Outfitted with hellfire missiles.

pod   just next to it   do you see it   yes   just west of
it   it's on the west side   descending crew   see a light

This sculpture of "Don Quijote de la Mancha" with spear and shield stands just north of the intersection of 2nd Street and Girard Avenue, which was once considered the entryway to Philadelphia's barrio. There are rumors that the neighbors didn't appreciate it when it was installed in 1997, as it promoted a European version of Spanishness, not connected to the realities of this location.

flash across   you do see the rectangular building next to it, correct?   yes sir that's affirmative   it's a mosque

You open the newspaper and skim the headlines. There are troops and there are cars exploding. There are marines and generals and presidents. You can hear coffee cups clicking on and off saucers behind you. There's a ceiling fan turning. A radio announces stock losses. Did you forget something very important, left behind on the nightstand? A very important name? A very important number?

do not engage the mosque   roger   the square building
is the mosque or is it the   the rectangle the rectangle!

The plaque on the base of the Don Quixote sculpture, obscured by overgrown rose bushes and inhabited by many birds, states that the statue (a copy of a sculpture by Joaquin Garcia Donaire made in 1967) was given as a gift by Ciudad Real in Spain "as a token of friendship and understanding between our two cultures."

roger that   ok in front of the mosque there are three
vehicles   do you see that   one of the vehicles is

What to do in the face of information uncertainty. Can you see your opponent across the way? Through the brush, behind the tree, across the street, in an unmarked car? Are you in a movie or standing still? As you put the items in the cart, you check them off the list. There's a security camera by the register and a mirrored wall at the back near the ceiling. You try to be "just atmosphere," prevent yourself from looking around. You act as if this is all you are here for. Left. Four steps. Right. Ten steps.

moving right now   you're cleared to engage it   do not

engage just monitor   roger   bring it up to channel p

Don Quixote was a man who saw a glorified fantasy in place of the real. In an historical twist, this character who saw windmills as oppressive giants or evil enchanters became a national symbol. He was figured as an ideal and then given as a gift. A gift by a royal city named "Real," to be received by a community that considers the offering out of synch with its own reality. A lively distortion, a funhouse mirror.

elevation   you are now cleared to engage the moving
vehicle   any personnel around you see   yes there are

Stealth over tempo? You're at the beginning. A fence signals a roadblock and a checkpoint. Tempo over numerical strength? You keep watch, control the traffic, everything is not normal so don't get too comfortable. A passerby who refuses to play may be at risk on the way to work, the movies, the bank machine. You notice something across the way. Has it always been there, or is this something new?

personnel   clear to engage those also   affirmative
let's go   confirm   [breathing]   two or three armed

When Don Quixote looks around him, at this broken down intersection, does he see the same golden palaces and bounteous treasures that the real estate (real city) developers pursue?

Does he see in his peripheral vision, the billboard to his right? The maiden Dulcinea? The king and his crown?

hey! ready!   good shot   direct secondaries   people
running through grass   more people   cleared to engage

Photo by Petty Officer 1st Class Bart A. Bauer

Sometimes on the job you imagine yourself as a chess piece. You report your coordinates then receive a new set for the day. You are the knight. You are the rook. You are the shah. You are the asp. Lay your horse's head down on this wide base. Let your flesh yield to the carved abstract. The phone rings, you pick it up, you say hello. You look into the camera and follow the instruction to look like you know what you're doing. Focus on a street sign, a brick wall. A thing among things.

all those   copy   hey! ready!   moving   come back
on those guys   there we got another   I've got people

Stretching from Logan Circle to the foot of the Benjamin Franklin Parkway, three sculptures trigger a triangle of looks.

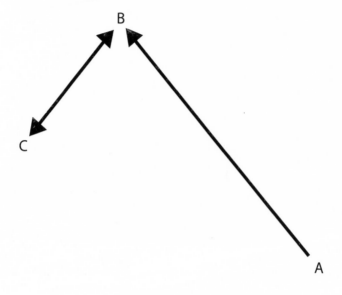

coming out of the mosque right now   hey!   ready!
secondaries   no secondaries   vehicles   guys are

The All Wars Memorial to Colored Soldiers and Sailors (A) depicts six black military men. Although they represent participation in "the various wars engaged in by the United States of America" up until 1934, they all wear WWI uniforms. They gather at the sides of a white woman ("the goddess of justice").

There are two infantrymen at the end of the row with rifles standing. They look out across the Parkway, past a flag of Slovenia, to the construction site that will soon be the new home for the Albert Barnes Collection. They watch it all the way to impact.

going to town man   personnel   running   there you go
move that further   hey!   ready!   watch out for that

Albert Barnes made his fortune in the early 20th century by developing a treatment for gonorrhea called Argyrol. In the 1920s he began to collect French Impressionist paintings, early works by Picasso, Soutine, Modigliani, and African art. The Barnes Foundation, dedicated to art education through "unmediated" contact with these works of art, opened in a Philadelphia suburb in 1922. But that contact was restricted; until very recently, the collection's works never left the building Barnes had built for them, and the public could visit only two days a week.

In 1925 Barnes published an article called "Negro Art and America," which praised the emotional vitality of "the primitive nature" and bemoaned the white man's habit of letting "the mind dominate the spirit." Their outer skin has no metal.

vehicle   kill truck flares   no joy load   continue
engaging   get that person   that's the flare pilot

In the late 1940s, Barnes struck up a friendship with the president of Lincoln University. Lincoln, located about 40 miles south of Barnes' collection, was founded in 1854 and was the first college dedicated solely to the education of African American students (Langston Hughes graduated in the class of 1929). In his will, Barnes gave Lincoln University all the seats on his foundation's board.

As the years passed, the Barnes endowment shrank and the collection was no longer able to sustain itself. A deal was brokered that freed Lincoln from the financial burden of maintaining the collection, and that led to the controversial approval to move the collection from the suburbs to a Center City location. As of 2010, while the new home for the artwork is being built, the controversy around the move rages on. The infantrymen take it in. No need to face their quarry.

that's the correct jump   just give me ten seconds   hey!
ready!   roger it went down to the ground   he just dove

The location of the All Wars Memorial to Colored Soldiers and Sailors was also a matter of controversy. After a Parkway placement was rejected, the sculpture was installed and dedicated in 1934 in an obscure and rarely visited corner of Fairmount Park. A campaign to relocate it to a more prominent spot asked donors to be "willing to re-write Philadelphia's history." In 1994, the sculpture was finally moved to its originally proposed site at the foot of the Ben Franklin Parkway.

If the two infantrymen pointed their rifles to follow their gaze, a vinyl fence screen with a quotation from Barnes would sit in their gunsights: "Renoir painted everything in the world in terms of fluid grace, beautiful flowers, blue skies, precious stones."

If they shifted their gaze just slightly to the left, the figures crowding the Civil War Soldiers and Sailors Memorial (B) would be the target of their aim. They track the heat signatures and fire.

on the ground   he's loaded   moving back to the
vehicles   personnel right there   hey!   ready!   hey!

The 1970s sculpture of the 18th-century Venezuelan general Francisco de Miranda (C) also aims his stare at the 19th-century soldiers. Glances ricochet from A to B to C in a pinball circuit of military histories.

Early in his career, Francisco de Miranda shipped off to Spain and bought himself a captainship. He soon became disenchanted with the Spanish army and dropped out. While traveling the world, he had an affair with Catherine the Great in Russia and private meetings with Thomas Jefferson and James Madison in the United States. After fighting to free Spain's American colonies (and failing to do so), he fought in the French Revolution. He was then invited by Simon Bolivar to again try freeing Venezuela from Spain. Miranda ended up signing an armistice, and Bolivar turned him in for treason. He spent his last days in a Spanish prison. Spun up and then called back.

> ready   you're going to get him   watch that mosque
> over there   roger   he went into the mosque   vehicles

Through the various twists and turns of time passing, Miranda became a Venezuelan hero rather than a traitor. He is known as "the precursor."

This sculpture was a Bicentennial gift to Philadelphia from the general consul of Venezuela. Miranda is about to pull his sword out of his sheath, his stone cape flapping in the wind. In the 1780s, he and the Marquis de Lafayette belonged to the same Masonic lodge. A statue of Lafayette—also depicted with cape swirling—can be found just a few blocks away, behind the Philadelphia Museum of Art.

They can see around corners and over hills; they'd like to get back in the air.

go to the building to put the 105s in standby   wildfire
we're cleared on the building cleared on the big square

Commissioned during WWI and installed in 1921, the Civil War Soldiers and Sailors Memorial (B) consists of two looming pylons. The soldiers take up the base of one, the sailors another across the way; together they form a gateway. Under the dispassionate scrutiny of (A) and (C), nine soldiers tangle around a cannon, clumsy and cramped. One holds a rifle and looks to Miranda (C) with resolve. One points his rifle ready to shoot above this inscription:

> . . . Each for himself gathered up the cherished purposes of life, its arms and desires, its dearest affections, and flung all with life itself into the scale of battle.

They breathe a lively target sparked with infrared.

building   go ahead and level it   roger that   clear that
building guys   roger   are you there   target   stay in

with thickened blood, metallic skin, and granite
breath, you look to the screen and see:

the area   check on vehicles too   personnel in the area
don't see any right now   hey!   ready!   offsetting

possible new target   approaching target one building
designate new target   target five   pilot copies   sensor

hey!   ready!   uh-oh   he fell   he's trying to lead
them   now if you go directly west approximately 100

you'd like to get back in the air, but you are adding to the
mission in this crucial way. you stay with the program.

you are committed to your job. you are a patch-wearer.
can you hide the sounds of your propellers? you map out

a rescue plan on a bar napkin. you watch it all the way to
impact. it's like data entry. you wind up and throw it in

with marble eye, static tongue, and frozen
fingers, you monitor the scene:

meters you'll see a single hotspot there, that's the cave
or tunnel entrance   hey!   ready!   try again   cleared to

fire   standby   ok you're in the box   rock em down
just fire   direct hit right there   hey!   ready!   not

certain   could be a howitzer   guy's moving guy's
moving   got him   no box no box   they're coming out

the air. a raven. outfitted with hellfire missiles. it needs
to be nimble. the streaming data while you chat via

keyboard. you are the sensor. enter coordinates and see
its airspace. using a joystick on a high hilltop. half-way

around the world and ordinarily a mess hall cook. sitting
in a trailer just outside las vegas. suited up. you throw the

with mineral heart, concrete lungs, and
clotted nerves, you check the visuals:

there you got it   hey!   ready!   see the other guy
yup   back on the other guys   already got that other guy

that one's still crawling there   ok   still moving
the one up to the south   yes!   hey!   ready!   left side

holed up and   look around here   I know those two
guys   I saw them flying apart   yeah I got that guy too

bird up when you want to throw it. you can see around corners and over hills; a god's eye view. it flattens the org

chart. is it a plane, a camera, or a gun. no need to face your quarry. drop your payload and fly off. your outer

skin has no metal. the belly is a rotating sphere of optics. in the clouds, no fixed orbit. fly a hexagon. fly a

With limestone hip, unsituated brain, and
motionless cells, you lock on:

I saw him die earlier   he was a 40 round direct   hey!
ready!   that guy's moving   yeah he is   he went down

that embankment   he was protected   direct hit   hey!
ready!   don't see anything moving   permission to go

back to compound   yeah go ahead and head back
to the compound

racetrack. fly a bowtie. who operates the ball? the screens
sweep you into the world. you give the customer what he

wants. an aerial stakeout. you get spun up and then called
back. you track the heat signatures and create a narrative.

spark the target in infrared. you're above the weather.
everything relies on visual confirmation, action no longer

sensation.

Acknowledgments

Thanks to Homay King and Jonathan Skinner for help taking photographs. Thanks to Amze Emmons for help with the maps and with everything. Thanks to Thalia Field as always. Thanks to Rob Armstrong, Margot Berg, Laura Griffith, Torben Jenk, and Andy Waskie for help with historical research. Thanks to Pia Simig, Lucy Douglas, and the Estate of Ian Hamilton Finlay. Thanks to Malcolm and Sam Holzman. Thanks to Donald Pfanz, staff historian at the Fredericksburg and Spotsylvania National Military Park. Thanks to the many excellent questions and comments after earlier versions of this work were presented at the Zinc Bar Reading/Talk series, the University of Pennsylvania Humanities Forum, the Moles Not Molars reading series at Nexus Gallery, the Center for Humanities at Temple University, Moore College of Art, Eyebeam Gallery, the Visual Culture Colloquium at Bryn Mawr College, the Verse Poetry Festival at the Georgia Museum of Art, the "Poetry Is News: Aesthetics of Common Ground" gathering at the Bowery Poetry Club, the Wesleyan Humanities Forum, Oberlin College, the Pennsylvania Academy of Fine Arts, Muhlenberg College, and Virginia Wesleyan College. Thanks to Suzanna Tamminen and Bronwyn Becker.

Early and partial versions of this work were published in *American Letters & Commentary*, *Vlak*, and *LAB Magazine*. An online Flash version was created by John Sparrow and is available in the online journal *HOW2* (vol. 3, no. 1). Thanks to the editors.

Photo Credits

Photos of sculptures in Philadelphia were taken by Jena Osman.

Photo of Ian Hamilton Finlay's "Wave" by Philip Hunter and photo of Finlay's "Man with Panzerschreck" by Antonia Reeve. Both used with the permission of the Estate of Ian Hamilton Finlay and the photographers.

Photo of Zouave soldier, courtesy of the National Park Service.

Use of the Max Becherer photo granted by Polaris. The caption for this photo on Becherer's website (www.maxbecherer.com) is quite different from that written by the *New York Times*:

> U.S. soldiers, with the 1st Battalion, 24th Infantry Regiment, Bravo Company, question a man charged with being part of a mortar and improvised explosive device team in the Islah Zeral neighborhood of Mosul. U.S. and Iraqi Army forces raided his home and detained four other men after receiving a tip from Iraqi Army intelligence. The soldiers hoped that the detained men would lead them to their mortars but they did not. The men were taken into Iraqi Army custody and then later released to U.S. custody. One of the men detained was a Master Sergeant in Saddam Hussein's Republican Guard, trained as a mortar man. A Mosul police station, called Four West, had received forty to fifty well-targeted rounds in the last few months by this team of men.

Photos of U.S. soldiers are considered fair use and were taken from the U.S. Army public-relations website in 2005: www.army.mil/search/images. The website asks that photographers be credited.

Sources

Albert Barnes, "Negro Art and America," *Survey Graphic*, March 1925.

Charles Baudelaire, "The Painter of Modern Life," in *The Painter of Modern Life and Other Essays*, ed. and trans. Jonathan Mayne (London: Phaidon Press, 1964).

Walter Benjamin, *The Arcades Project*, ed. Rolf Tiedemann and trans. Howard Eiland and Kevin McLaughlin (Cambridge: Harvard University Press, 2002):

> It's not that what is past casts its light on what is present, or what is present its light on what is past; rather image is that wherein what has been comes together in a flash with the now to form a constellation. In other words, image is dialectics at a standstill. For while the relation of the present to the past is a purely temporal, continuous one, the relation of what-has-been to the now is dialectical: is not progression but image, suddenly emergent.—Only dialectical images are genuine images (that is, not archaic); and the place where one encounters them is language. [N2a, 3]

Russell Conwell, "Acres of Diamonds," www.temple.edu/about/AcresofDiamonds.htm.

Dexter Filkins, "Where the Shadows Have Shadows," *New York Times*, February 5, 2006 (with photo by Max Becherer).

Godey's Lady's Book, November 1859 (for Zouave jacket).

Earl Goldsmith's Spirit of the American Doughboy database, http://doughboysearcher.weebly.com/the-spirit-of-the-american-doughboy.html.

Francisco Goya, *Disasters of War*, c. 1810–15.

Philadelphia Public Art Database, www.philart.net.

Rosalind Kraus, "Sculpture in the Expanded Field," in *The Anti-Aesthetic: Essays on Postmodern Culture*, ed. Hal Foster (Port Townsend, WA: Bay Press, 1983), 31-42.

Robert Musil, "Monuments," in *Selected Writings*, ed. Burton Pike (New York: Continuum, 1986).

George Oppen, "Of Being Numerous," in *New Directions* (New York: New Directions, 1968).

Smithsonian Inventory of American Sculpture, http://siris-artinventories.si.edu.

Susan Stewart, "Garden Agon," *Representations*, no. 62 (Spring 1998): 111–43.

Drone text is transcribed from various videos found on YouTube.